Chicken Soup for the Soul.

Saved by an Angel

Amy Newmark

CSS

Chicken Soup for the Soul, LLC
Cos Cob, CT

Chicken Soup for the Soul: Saved by an Angel
Amy Newmark

Published by Chicken Soup for the Soul, LLC www.chickensoup.com

The publisher gratefully acknowledges the many publishers and individuals who granted Chicken Soup for the Soul permission to reprint the cited material.

Front cover photo courtesy of Getty Images/Richard Newstead, Lifesize. Back cover and interior photo courtesy of Photos.com/Musat (© Christian Musat)

Interior photo of Amy Newmark courtesy of Susan Morrow at SwickPix

Cover and Interior by Daniel Zaccari

ISBN: 978-1-61159-058-6

PRINTED IN THE UNITED STATES OF AMERICA
on acid∞free paper

25 24 23 22 21   04 05 06 07 08 09 10 11

Table of Contents

An Unlikely Protector

*It is not because angels are holier than men
or devils that makes them angels, but because
they do not expect holiness from one another,
but from God alone.*
~William Blake

I n early 2001, our daughter Elizabeth was determined to take a bus trip from Iowa to Ohio to meet the young man she'd been writing to for several years. Her father and I weren't very happy with her decision and were especially worried about the many stops in larger cities, but she dismissed our concerns. She was eighteen, had saved up enough money to make the trip, and nothing we said could dissuade her.

When we dropped her off at the bus stop, we hugged her tightly and warned her to be very careful. As the bus pulled away, I found myself saying a prayer for her safe arrival.

That very night, we watched a police drama where a young girl's body was found behind a dumpster at a bus station. "An innocent Iowa girl, raped and murdered," one police offer lamented to the other, after they discovered her identity. My blood ran cold. I looked up to see a matching fear in David's eyes. We were thinking the same thing: We shouldn't have let her go.

Neither one of us got much sleep that long night, tossing and turning and reaching out for each other's hands. Over and over, we prayed for our daughter, repeating the same prayer I'd uttered under my breath at the bus stop: Please Lord, take care of our daughter on this journey. Watch over her.

I breathed a huge sigh of relief when Elizabeth finally called the next afternoon to say she'd arrived at her destination. I told her about the television program the night before, expecting her to tell me I was silly for worrying. Instead there was silence at the other end.

Then my daughter began telling me about the five-hour layover she had at 3:00 a.m., at a bus station that consisted of little more than a single locked building in the middle of nowhere. Just as she approached the door of the structure, a hulk of a man with long stringy hair and bulging tattooed biceps appeared from a nearby alley.

My terrified daughter twisted the doorknob back and forth frantically, to no avail. It was locked tight and there were no lights on inside.

Shoulders slumped in resignation, she did the only thing she could think to do; she sat down on her suitcase and began praying in earnest. She kept her eyes to the ground, trying to avoid eye contact with the fearsome stranger as he approached her.

When she finally dared to look up, the man was standing right in front of her. When he greeted her, she gulped back her fear enough to whisper a shaky hello. As he attempted to strike up a casual conversation, she bravely responded with one-word answers. He stood uncomfortably close to her as he talked. He asked her where she was headed and told her about the girlfriend he was headed to Florida to visit. She gradually relaxed as she realized that despite his rough exterior and language, he meant her no harm.

During the two hours that they stood alone outside, my daughter noticed at least three different vehicles filled with groups of young men drive by, one car circling at least twice. The men looked at my daughter, and then glanced at the big man standing next to her. None of them stopped.

By 5:15 a woman with a ring full of keys arrived, and as she opened the door to the station, Elizabeth heard the man mumble something, disappearing back into the alley. The attendant allowed her to enter the building, despite the fact that it wouldn't officially open for another fifteen minutes.

Once Elizabeth was locked inside, the man returned

and tried to open the door. My daughter called out to him that the station wouldn't open until 5:30, and he nodded and walked away. She never saw him again.

Elizabeth waited inside the station for almost three hours, but never saw the man come into the building or get on a bus.

"Mom, if he hadn't been there and one of those cars full of guys stopped, they could have done anything to me. I would have been totally alone in the middle of the night. I could have been that girl in the show you watched."

I gasped in shock, but then Elizabeth added, "Mom, where did he go? The station wasn't crowded. If he really had planned to get on a bus, why did he disappear once I was safe inside?"

I felt a warm sense of peace fill me. I knew then, without a doubt, that God had answered my prayers by sending that burly bodyguard to watch over my daughter. "He was God's angel," I told Elizabeth, but she wasn't so sure.

"He didn't look like an angel, or talk like an angel,"

she responded uncertainly.

"If he had looked less intimidating, would his presence have hindered any of those cars from stopping?"

Beth went quiet as we both considered what might have happened if that formidable-looking man hadn't been standing so protectively close to her.

Were it not for that fortuitous encounter at the closed bus station, Elizabeth might not have made it as far as Ohio to meet the young man who would eventually become her husband and the father of her three children.

I know for a fact that angels exist, though we might not always recognize them when they visit us. Sometimes God's angel can be a big, burly man with tattooed arms.

~Mary Potter Kenyon

An Angel of Calm

The magnitude of life is overwhelming.
Angels are here to help us take it
peace by peace.
~Levende Waters

Going to school during my older brother's intense six-year battle with drug abuse was an ordeal in itself — hiding my distress daily from friends, pretending to be carefree. It should have been over after he died. But the stress of his murder highly suspected to be at the hands of a dealer eight months earlier had left me even more anxiety-ridden. Especially the day that my best friend begged me to accept a ride home from her after school. I could see tension in her hands as she fumbled for her keys. What a pair we were. If ever two young girls needed a miracle, it was us.

Mandy had driven her family's blue boat of a car to school on her own as she occasionally did. "I can't take long," she said, in her usual nerve-wracked manner, "but you're really on the way...." Then, almost like a whispered afterthought, "My mother said it was okay."

I tried to mask my shudder. What would happen if Mandy got home a few minutes late?

Mandy was such a different person inside the walls of school. Laughing, talkative, caring. But no sooner would the final bell ring than she'd begin a slow, distracted freeze—a tightening of her body as she'd grip her books to her chest and race, stumbling, out to a car waiting at the curb. It didn't matter if we were in the middle of a conversation coming out of class. She'd get that fearful look and rush out.

Often, I watched Mandy jump into the car, hanging her head low. The driver appeared to be chewing her out for taking too long, flashing angry eyes and waving her hands in Mandy's face.

Connecting the dots I realized poor Mandy was being abused, at least verbally.

Not wanting to hurt her feelings, I slid in the passenger seat even though I was nervous about accepting a ride from such a new driver—and a jittery one at that. But what could happen in just two miles?

Mandy backed out of the school parking lot and pulled out at the light. It seemed like we were moving at a snail's pace, but I was glad she was cautious. Carefully, she swung left from the busy boulevard onto the side street leading to my neighborhood. At that moment, from nowhere, a car was coming straight at us!

"Mandy!" I cried at the splintering sound of two cars colliding head-on, rocking us backward. We'd barely been going—what, fifteen miles an hour? Still, we sat there, stunned.

Mandy gripped the wheel, her face and knuckles

white as snow. "Wh-what d-do I d-do?" she whispered. I stared back.

I had no idea. I didn't even drive. What do you do when someone hits your car? Did we have to call the police? (This was pre-cell phone days, and we'd have had to bang on a stranger's door to call anyone.)

The other driver slammed out of his car, irritation darkening his face. I could run home, I thought wildly… get Mom… but Dad had our only car at work. Poor Mandy began to shake. It wasn't her fault. But how could we prove it?

Just then, an urgent knocking on Mandy's window made us jump. She lowered the window, where a man not involved in the accident had suddenly appeared. Dressed like a businessman, his expression was calm. Confidently, he patted Mandy's hand still on the wheel. "It's okay," he comforted her. "Don't worry. I've talked to the other driver and he knows it's his fault. Neither of you has much damage."

Mandy looked up at him wordlessly, focusing

as if on a lifeline. Tall and strong looking, his words and manner made me strangely calm. The sudden peace inside the car seemed almost otherworldly.

"Here's what you need to do," he said, explaining step by step how to obtain the other driver's insurance, information she should get and give, what to look for in her glove compartment. Flashing her one more assuring smile, he repeated, "Don't worry."

The two of us opened the doors and stepped out. Quietly, Mandy began talking with the other driver. Things seemed to be going smoothly enough and Mandy had stopped shaking. It had only been a moment when I turned to thank the man who had advised us, but—glancing up and down the street—I could find no one around. Anywhere. No other cars were on the street and there was no activity at any of the houses.

Come to think of it, I hadn't seen or heard any cars besides Mandy's and the other driver. Never heard any doors shut anywhere, or even footsteps. And—I wondered then—when had he had time to talk to the other driver before us?

Soon we were on our way and pulling into my driveway. Mom greeted us at the door, where the story spilled out. "Stay for tea, honey," Mom urged her. "You could use a minute before you get going."

Certain she'd refuse, I was amazed to find Mandy follow us in and take a seat in the wing chair. Cradling steaming cups in our hands, we were silent.

"Mandy," I said thoughtfully. "Did you notice… that man just… disappeared?"

She nodded, slowly.

"Girls," Mom said, "I think God sent you an angel today."

Tears pooled in Mandy's eyes and I could feel that same choking back I always felt when I watched my favorite movie, *It's A Wonderful Life*. Especially in the moment when little Zuzu tells Jimmy Stewart about every time a bell rings. "That's right, honey!" he'd exclaim exuberantly. "That's right!"

That afternoon, Mom called Mandy's mother and smoothed the way for her to stay and talk over cookies for a bit. It was the first of many days when she would somehow manage to steal away to spend an hour or so with us after school. I never knew all of what she confided to Mom, but soon Mandy moved in with a beloved grandma who had been praying for her all along. Since that day of the accident, we both had fresh hope in new beginnings.

Sometimes, I'd walk down that street coming home from school, looking in open garages or doorways, just to make sure. But I never saw him again. Something in me knew. He had been no ordinary man.

The memory of his reassuring, calm presence, framed in the window behind Mandy's white-knuckled grip, reminds me that God cares personally about our sorrows and fears. So deeply that He still sends his angels as He did in the Bible. And they still have the same message. Do not worry. God is with you.

~Pam Depoyan

Angels Don't Need Your Address

The golden moments in the stream of life
rush past us and we see nothing but sand;
the angels come to visit us, and we only know
them when they are gone.
~George Eliot

I t was a typical last weekend of summer mania at the beach, and of course I wanted to be part of the madness. My husband thought that a quiet barbeque at home would suffice. But given his gentle and accommodating ways, there we were lying supine on our rainbow-striped towels like sardines in a tin. If we inched forward, backward, left or right, we would be quite intimate with our beach neighbors.

I was thrilled to hear the ocean roar, feel the mist on my face, taste the saltiness in the air. My husband said he could have easily duplicated this experience back home by playing one of those new wave CDs in the background (the ones that sound like a combination of an eerie violin and waterfalls) while he sprayed me with a mister and fed me potato chips.

I put him under the umbrella and headed for one of my famous beach adventures. Seashell collecting followed by a hunt for sea glass, a walk along the jetty and the ultimate reward — wading, dipping, diving and eventually riding back in on my own private wave.

We headed home, sun-drenched and parched and in dire need of showers. And that's when I noticed that my owl necklace, a thirtieth birthday gift given to me by my dad just one week before he passed away, was not where it should have been and always was: hanging right below the I Love

You necklace given to me by my husband on our wedding night.

My two most favorite men on the planet and my two most treasured gifts, and now one was missing. I was frantic as I searched every room in the house. I asked my husband if he recalled seeing the necklace on me while we were at the beach. He couldn't be sure and neither could I.

All I could be certain of was that I was heartbroken.

I grabbed the car keys and headed back to the beach. My husband thought I was crazy and rightly so. Nine miles of beach, thirty thousand beachgoers later—did I really think I could locate one teeny necklace?

I knew I had to try. At least there was a Lost and Found. Maybe, just maybe, someone came across my necklace and turned it in. Then cynically I thought, maybe, just maybe with the price of gold someone did not.

What if it came off in the ocean?

I was unwilling to even consider that as a

possibility.

I rushed onto the beach and didn't know where to begin. The lifeguards were long gone but a worker sweeping the boardwalk had access to the Lost and Found. One deck of playing cards, three beach chairs, and more than six coolers were stacked along the wall but no necklace anywhere.

I noticed an elderly man slowly walking the sand with a metal detector in his hand. I raced up to him and, nearly breathless, asked if he had come across a necklace.

He opened his yellowed weather-beaten hand and showed me his bounty thus far—nickels and quarters but mostly pennies.

The old man said I could write down my name and address and if he happened to come upon my necklace he would gladly return it to me. I wanted to hug him so I did.

I also wanted him to have sufficient postage to mail it back to me so I gave him a crumpled up $5 bill that he re-crumpled and put in his vest pocket.

I raced back to my car to find something to write with (and on) and found a dull-tipped eyebrow pencil and a napkin.

I scribbled my name and address and ran back as fast as I could.

The old man was gone.

I searched for a while and then went home.

My generous husband offered to replace the little blue owl with a new one.

I turned down his loving gesture, as there could be no replacement. My dad, despite being hospitalized for the better part of seven months, had found a way to buy me that necklace and not miss my thirtieth birthday. I had learned about it at his funeral.

There had been a fundraising event in the lobby of the hospital a few days earlier where merchants were selling their wares. Having gotten wind of this, my dad had asked one of the orderlies if he could wheel him downstairs.

On display in a small white box on a corner table he spotted the owl necklace and knew he had found the very best gift of all. My dad always told me how wise I was, even as a little girl, wise beyond my years he would say. Wise like a wise old owl.

Without money to pay for the owl, my dad had to barter with the vendor. He offered to build something in his occupational therapy class like a magazine rack or a wooden boat in exchange for my birthday gift.

The vendor gave my dad the owl with an IOU and Dad's favorite nurse brought it home to gift-wrap as though it had come from Tiffany.

I would later learn that this kind vendor had just lost his father to cancer and was so moved by my dad's gumption and dignity that he never had any intention of accepting any money.

Three days after combing the beach for the fourth and final time a package appeared inside our screen door.

I don't know who delivered it or who sent it, as there was no return address nor any postage of any kind.

Inside was a crumpled up $5 bill and my owl necklace.

First I cried.

Then I kissed that beautiful owl.

Then I put my necklace back on where it belonged.

And only then did I realize how silly I had been.

I never needed to worry about writing down where I lived. Angels don't need your address.

~Lisa Leshaw

Daniel and the Pelican

*If we were all like angels, the world would be
a heavenly place.*
~Author Unknown

As I drove home from work one afternoon, the cars ahead of me were swerving to miss something not often seen in the middle of a six-lane highway: a great big pelican. After an eighteen-wheeler nearly ran him over, it was clear the pelican wasn't planning to move any time soon. And if he didn't, the remainder of his life could be clocked with an egg timer.

I parked my car and slowly approached him. The bird wasn't the least bit afraid of me, and the drivers who honked their horns and yelled at us as they sped by didn't impress him either.

Stomping my feet, I waved my arms and shouted to get him into the lake next to the road, all the while trying to direct traffic.

"C'mon beat it, Big Guy, before you get hurt!"

After a brief pause, he cooperatively waddled to the curb and slid down to the water's edge.

Problem solved. Or so I thought.

The minute I walked away he was back on the road, resulting in another round of honking, squealing tires and smoking brakes.

So I tried again.

"Shoo, for crying out loud!"

The bird blinked, first one eye then the other, and with a little sigh placated me by returning to the lake.

Of course when I started for my car it was instant replay.

After two more unsuccessful attempts, I was at my wits' end. Cell phones were practically non-existent back then, and the nearest pay phone was about a mile away. I wasn't about to abandon the hapless creature and run for help. He probably wouldn't be alive when I returned.

So there we stood, on the curb, like a couple of folks waiting at a bus stop. While he nonchalantly preened his feathers, I prayed for a miracle.

Suddenly a shiny red pickup truck pulled up, and a man hopped out.

"Would you like a hand?"

I'm seldom at a loss for words, but one look at the very tall newcomer rendered me tongue-tied and unable to do anything but nod.

He was the most striking man I'd ever seen—smoky black hair, muscular with tanned skin, and a tender smile flanked by dimples deep enough to drill for oil. His eyes were hypnotic, crystal clear and Caribbean blue. He was almost too beautiful to be real.

The embroidered name on his denim work shirt said "Daniel."

"I'm on my way out to the Seabird Sanctuary, and I'd be glad to take him with me. I have a big cage in the back of my truck," the man offered.

Oh my goodness.

"Do you volunteer at the Sanctuary?" I croaked, struggling to regain my powers of speech.

"Yes, every now and then."

In my wildest dreams, I couldn't have imagined a more perfect solution to my dilemma. The bird was going to be saved by a knowledgeable expert with movie star looks, who happened to have a pelican-sized cage with him and was on his way to the Seabird Sanctuary.

As I watched Daniel prepare for his passenger, I couldn't shake the feeling that I knew him from somewhere.

"Have we ever met before?" I asked.

"No I don't think so," was his reply, smiling again with warmth that would melt glaciers.

I held my breath as the man crept toward the pelican. Their eyes met, and the bird meekly allowed

Daniel to drape a towel over his face and place him in the cage. There was no struggle, no flapping wings and not one peep of protest—just calm.

"Yes!" I shrieked with excitement when the door was latched. What had seemed a no-win situation was no longer hopeless. The pelican was finally safe.

Before they drove away, I thanked my fellow rescuer for his help.

"It was my pleasure, Michelle."

And he was gone.

Wait a minute. How did he know my name? We didn't introduce ourselves. I only knew his name because of his shirt.

Later when I called the Sanctuary to check on the pelican, I asked if I might speak with Daniel.

No one had ever heard of him.

I was beginning to think my mind was playing tricks on me.

As we discussed my baffling experience over dinner, our little girl Julie was convinced that she knew Daniel's true identity.

"Mommy, I'll bet he's your angel. That's why you know him," she insisted.

"But Daniel didn't have wings, honey." I smiled, passing the green beans to my husband.

"A lot of angels don't have wings, Mommy."

"How do you know this?"

"I see them sometimes. They're just people like you, me and Daddy."

I put down my fork and gave her my full attention.

"Julie, why do you think the people you see are angels?" I asked.

"Because God is in their faces."

After dishes were washed and bedtime prayers were said, it was time to sort through the confusion whirling through my head.

I read somewhere that young children are able to see what adults can't because their innocence hasn't yet been tainted by the skepticism of a grownup world. It must be true. My baby daughter seemed to have the inside track on something her incredulous mother could barely comprehend.

Moreover what she said made sense.

I prayed for a miracle and Daniel suddenly appeared. He not only knew how to capture a pelican, but had a big cage in his truck and was on his way to a place where the bird would be safe.

And the glow radiating from Daniel's beautiful eyes was pure and loving, like the adoration of a father for his child. As Julie said, God was in his face.

If Daniel was my angel it would explain his familiarity. My spirit might know him even if I didn't recognize him in the flesh. And he'd know my name without being told.

Then I recalled struggling to hold back traffic while trying to get the pelican off the road. Perhaps the bird wasn't the only one in imminent danger. I was so preoccupied that it didn't occur to me that I was in danger of losing my own life while trying to save his.

It was a precious and humbling revelation—to be so cherished by God that He would send one of the Heavenly hosts to protect me. I'd heard that angels watch over us, but I was handed tangible evidence of their existence.

What an amazing gift.

~Michelle Close Mills

Stranded

*Not all of us can do great things. But we can
do small things with great love.*
~Mother Teresa

My mind started wandering. I had been driving on I-79 North in our newly acquired used Jeep Cherokee with my pregnant wife through the mountains of West Virginia for nearly two hours. No radio. No cell phone service. No stop lights. No rest areas. No vehicles on the road other than ours. The only noise we heard was the slow drone of the wiper blades moving back and forth, reminding me of the metronome my fifth grade piano instructor used to keep me on tempo.

The slushy mix of snow, rain, and sleet started picking up, making it harder and harder to focus on the seemingly endless road before us.

It was the night before Christmas Eve and we were making the long trek home to rural Pennsylvania. I was attending graduate school in Kentucky and our winter break had finally arrived. My wife and I had to work earlier in the day so we got off to a later start than we would have liked—forcing us to drive in utter darkness the entire trip home. We didn't really mind the drive though, knowing that in eight hours we would be enjoying eggnog in front of a warm fireplace with our family.

BOOM!!!

"Did you hear that?" I asked my wife.

"Yes. What happened?"

"I must have hit something," I said.

I pulled the vehicle off to the side of the road to check out the damage. I grabbed the flashlight from under my seat.

"We got a flat!" I yelled. "I'm going to put on

the doughnut."

One by one I grabbed our Christmas presents, placing them on the sloppy ground. I finally made it the bottom of the pile, grabbing the jack, our only source of hope on this wintry night.

"Great, just our luck, it's broken! The car dealer sold us a vehicle with a broken jack! Now what?"

One by one I placed the saturated Christmas gifts back into the vehicle, replaying in my head how I could have made such a mistake. I returned to my seat and started wondering what our next move might be. We took a moment to assess the situation and offer up a quick prayer.

We laid out our options:

Option 1—It looked like there was a house way off in the distance. I could ring their doorbell.

Option 2—The next exit was fifteen miles. I could walk to the exit and my wife could stay in the car until I returned.

Option 3—We could wait it out in the warmth

of our car until the gas ran out—hoping that another vehicle would stop and perform a modern-day Good Samaritan deed on our behalf (even though we hadn't seen another car on the road for nearly two hours).

Neither one of us liked options one or two, considering the fact that we were in the middle of nowhere in West Virginia—so we decided on option three.

I reclined in my seat, not expecting to see another vehicle for several hours, if at all. I shut off the wiper blades so I could have a normal conversation with my wife. But before I uttered the first sentence, I heard what sounded like sirens. I looked in the rearview mirror and shouted as if I had just won the lottery: "A police car!"

The policeman pulled alongside our vehicle, asking us how he could be of service, telling us that his name was Officer Anderson. I told him about the flat tire and that we didn't have a working jack or cell phone service. Without hesitation, Officer

Anderson hopped out of his vehicle, grabbed the jack from his car, plopped down on the soggy grass, and started changing the tire. He then told us to stay inside where it was warm while he found us a mechanic. He eventually found us one, but it was forty-five miles away. He told us that he would follow behind us until we made it to our destination. So for the next hour and half, Officer Anderson followed behind our vehicle, even though it was way out of his jurisdiction.

When we finally arrived at our exit, Officer Anderson told us to follow him to the mechanic and that he would give us a ride to a hotel. Before he left, I felt compelled to ask him for his police station address so I could send him a proper thank you, and to ask him a question that I had been mulling over since the moment he stopped to help us several hours before:

"So why did you stop?"

After a long pause, he looked me directly in the eyes and said:

"I stopped to help you and your family because someone stopped and helped me and my family when we were in need many years ago."

Officer Anderson's words have been reverberating in my heart and mind ever since that night. His words (and actions) have provided me with much hope in my life when we have been in difficult situations and needed help—and there have been many. His words have also been the driving force behind my mission in this life—to reach out and help those who are in need, to those who are hurting, to those who need compassion, to those who need someone to help carry their burdens.

The truth of the matter is that we all need an Officer Anderson from time to time. Life gets challenging—a flat tire, a broken relationship, an unforeseen illness, a sudden job loss, or an unexpected bill to pay. But like Officer Anderson mentioned, he stopped and helped us because someone stopped to help him first.

The day after Christmas I decided to contact the police station to properly thank Officer Anderson for his service. The police chief answered and I started recounting the amazing act of kindness we had received from one of his officers. The police chief responded, "I'm very glad you received the help you needed the other night but there isn't an Officer Anderson at our station."

To this day I'm not sure if there really is an Officer Anderson who roams the mountains of West Virginia on I-79 north or if he is simply an angel, but I do know that this amazing act of kindness has drastically changed the course of my life.

~Tom Kaden

The Nick of Time

*Be an angel to someone else whenever you
can, as a way of thanking God for the help
your angel has given you.*
~Eileen Elias Freeman,
The Angels' Little Instruction Book

While many people believe that they are surrounded by angels and tell stories about angels having helped them out of tight spots, I must admit that I always fell on the more skeptical side whenever I heard about an angel encounter. Coincidence, I usually thought, when someone told me about how "their" angel lent them a hand. Good timing. Nothing more than being in the right place at the right time. Until, that is, I met an angel of my own.

It was 1990 and I was looking for a job. Not just hoping to find one, but pretty desperate to get something that would help pay the mortgage of the new house my husband and I had just bought. After answering an ad in the paper and landing an interview, I set off one bright winter morning, more than a little nervous, but dressed in my interviewing best to wow my potential boss.

My interview was in the downtown section of the city we had just moved to, and I was fairly certain that I knew how to get there. But to be safe, I gave myself an extra half hour.

Finding the building was a piece of cake, but what I hadn't counted on was having no place to park downtown in the middle of the morning on a busy Monday. The building was in the middle of a block filled with office buildings, restaurants and a few older houses, and every parking place I saw was already taken.

I circled the block several times, a feeling of panic rising in my chest every time I turned a corner. Although I'd allowed ample time to get to the interview, I hadn't factored in fruitlessly driving around downtown in search of parking.

As I slowly made my way down the street for what seemed like the hundredth time, I noticed a woman with flaming red hair standing at the end of a driveway, one hand on her hip and the other holding a broom she was using to sweep snow off her sidewalk. She waved at me and I slowed down.

"Are you lost?" she asked when I rolled down my window. "I've seen you go by half a dozen times at least."

"No, I'm not lost. I'm trying to find a spot to park. I have a job interview in five minutes in that building across the street."

The woman smiled sympathetically. "Park in my driveway," she offered. "I'm not going anywhere."

"Are you sure?" I asked.

"Of course I'm sure! And hurry! You don't want

to be late, do you?" The woman gestured toward a spot she'd just swept clear of snow and I gratefully pulled my car into her driveway. After thanking her again, I ran across the street and made it to my interview with a minute to spare. Afterwards I returned to get my car.

The red-haired woman was still outside sweeping. "How'd it go?" she asked.

"I think it went all right," I told her. "Thank you again for your help."

She smiled at me. "Isn't that what folks are supposed to do, be kind to each other? I hope you get the job."

That night I told my husband about the woman who'd offered me a parking spot in the nick of time. "I'd like to bring her something to thank her," I said. "Maybe a plant or some cookies. I'll take her something tomorrow."

The next morning, Tuesday, I drove back downtown, with a small African violet plant on the car seat next to me. For some reason there were plenty of parking spots that day and I was able to park directly in front of the generous stranger's house. But as I rang the front doorbell, there was no answer.

"No one lives there!" someone called out to me after a few minutes. A neighbor appeared on the steps of the house next door.

"Yesterday a woman who lived here let me park in her driveway," I replied.

The neighbor shook her head. "I don't think so. Helen went into a nursing home last month and she passed away on Sunday."

"Did Helen have red hair and blue eyes?"

"No. Helen had blue eyes but her hair was white. She was quite elderly. It must have been someone else." The neighbor started back into her house before stopping. "That's funny though. I think Helen did have red hair, a long time ago. She always said her hair used to be the same color as Lucille Ball's." The neighbor eyed the plant I was holding. "Nice violet," she said.

A shiver ran down my spine as I remembered

what Helen had said about being kind to each other. Walking over to the neighbor's house, I handed her the violet. "Enjoy," I told her. "I'd like you to have this."

Her eyes widened. "What for?"

Shrugging, I replied, "As a thank you to Helen."

Later that week I was offered the job, and for several years I drove past Helen's house twice a day. And every time I did, I thought about the angel I'd met and her kindness to me, kindness I still try to pass on to others whenever I can.

My encounter with Helen showed me that meeting an angel isn't about coincidences or good timing or being in the right place at the right time. It's about being kind to each other whenever we possibly can.

~Nell Musolf

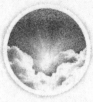

Roadside Assistance

*The LORD will command His loving kindness
in the daytime, and in the night His song shall
be with me—A prayer to the God of my life.*
~Psalm 42:8

It was a rainy Sunday summer afternoon and my friend and I had been driving for an hour. We drove quiet backcountry roads that took us past cow pastures and horse farms and not much else. We drove secluded dirt roads—not a home in view for miles. As we rounded another bend we passed, for the second time, the same roadside eatery we had passed twenty minutes earlier—the one with the "Closed" sign hanging in the door.

With our gas tank needle pointing towards "Empty" we resisted the temptation to pick up a serious-looking hitchhiker for the express purpose of having him assist us in finding our way. His countenance disturbed us, but just what it was about him that troubled us neither of us could pinpoint.

When we pulled into a gas station in the rural countryside of Lancaster County, Pennsylvania, we finally admitted to each other that we were, indeed, lost.

Before the age of technology—before GPS navigation and cell phones—there were road maps. Fortunately, we had a Pennsylvania map. We had just pulled it out of the glove compartment when a white car pulled into the gas station on the opposite side of the pumps.

Headed home after a five-day camping trip at a Christian music festival, my friend and I were anxious to get back to civilization that included hot showers and warm beds. My friend dutifully studied the map while I slid out of the driver's seat and made my way towards the office of the gas station.

I smiled and nodded at the people in the car next to ours—an elderly couple. The man driving the car had white hair and wore a white shirt. His wife also had white hair and had a white cardigan thrown across her shoulders. She held a happy-go-lucky white Poodle in her lap. The woman smiled back at me and nodded.

The elderly gentleman rolled down his window and called out, "You won't find anyone in there—the station's closed on Sunday."

"Oh, okay, thanks," I replied, disappointed. How foolish of me to think that I would find an open gas station in the middle of Amish country on a Sunday afternoon.

"I see you've got Jersey plates. Headed home? You missed your turn about three miles back. You should have turned right just after the stone mill."

"Oh—there were no signs. And... well... as a matter of fact, yes, we're headed back to New Jersey. We've been driving in circles for an hour."

"Well, good thing you didn't pick up that hitch-hiker back there. He's a troubled man," the elderly gentleman replied.

I looked over at my friend, whose mouth hung open in disbelief. With the map opened fully on her lap, she said in a low voice, "How did he know? There was no one following us on those roads and he pulled into this station from the opposite direction."

His next comment interrupted our discussion. "If you want to follow us, we'll get you back to the Interstate and then about two miles east there's a gas station where you can get some fuel."

I leaned into the driver's side window of the car. "How did you know we needed gas? And how did you know we were lost?"

"Well, let's just call it divine intervention," he quipped as he smiled. His wife chuckled and the Poodle stood at attention with his little tail straight up in the air. "I'll pull out of the station and you can follow us to the Interstate."

"We can't thank you enough. You are so kind.

Can I give you some money for the extra gas and for your trouble?" I asked.

"Oh no—that won't be necessary. We're only a few miles away and we're heading in that direction."

"Well thank you again." I smiled at them and slipped back into the car.

As we meandered through the countryside my friend and I speculated—could it be that these were angels sent to help us find our way and protect us? Could it all be just a coincidence—an elderly couple from the area, out for a Sunday afternoon drive, who came across two lost Jersey girls? Irrespective of who and why, we were thankful for their assistance.

As we made our way closer to the Interstate we saw the gentleman pull to the side of the road, roll down his window, and point at the exit we needed to take just ahead. We waved goodbye as we passed them and I used my turn signal to indicate I understood his directive. As we ascended the entry ramp to the highway my friend looked back to wave again. She gasped — the car was gone. "Look in your mirror," she instructed. Amazed and speechless, we headed home.

Later that night, lying in my cozy bed after a hot meal and a cool shower, I picked up my Bible and randomly opened to the book of Hebrews, Chapter 13. I began reading.

"Let brotherly love continue. Be not forgetful to entertain strangers: for thereby some have entertained angels unawares."

At that moment the events of the day became clear. Our escorts from earlier in the day were not strangers living in a lonely town in Lancaster County, Pennsylvania. I quickly called my friend to share with her the confirmation of our earlier suspicion — angels.

Today, in those moments when I become impatient with others, I remember that verse from Hebrews and recollect our experience. Would anyone ever believe us? Probably not, we surmised back then. We had encountered angels unaware who treated us with kindness and compassion. How could I ever do anything less?

~Elisa Yager

The Jolly Bus Driver

*Laughter is the shortest distance
between two people.*
~Victor Borge

I was sixteen years old and had enough money to buy a bus ticket out of town. Destination—my sister's house in Kellogg, a small mountain community in northern Washington state.

The bus ride would take me north through Walla Walla, Washington then on to Spokane. A snowstorm was underway but I wasn't worried. I had a few dollars in my pocket and the open road ahead of me.

The Greyhound lumbered out of the terminal.

I felt safe and warm snuggled up against the window. A rest from running away, I was living in the moment with no worry about what came next. I soon drifted off to sleep and didn't wake for some time. When I did wake up, the bus was stopped. Wiping the sleep from my eyes I looked around to see that I was the only one on the bus.

Shaking off the stiffness in my legs, I stood and walked down the aisle. Peering out the door I could see the small terminal. Through the darkness, I could barely read the snow-crusted sign above the door. Welcome to Walla Walla. Tired and hungry, I went back to my seat and snuggled down against the cold. The driver came back on the bus. I heard his rough voice bellow at me.

"Hey, you down there!"

"Oh crap," I whispered, shrinking down further in the seat.

"You seem to be the only passenger going on, young lady. You better go in and warm up. I doubt if we are going any further tonight."

I didn't move; I just slumped more in the seat. "Suit yourself," he snapped.

I was in no mood to make a new plan and found myself choking back the lump that had formed in my throat. "Don't cry," I told myself. "Nobody is going to see me cry." It was then he stepped on the bus. He was dressed in a bus driver uniform with a funny old-fashioned cap. He looked like Santa Claus—a big man with a white beard and suspenders that wrapped around his round belly.

"Might as well come sit up front, young lady. Looks like you are the only one going on to Spokane," he said. Slowly I made my way to the front of the bus. "Might as well take that front row seat," he laughed.

Cautiously I sat down in the front row seat across from him. The biggest flakes I had ever seen blanketed the window.

Off we went into that blizzard, just me and the jolly bus driver. It was odd for me to take such a chance. I remember thinking that this could turn out bad. As I sat staring into the darkness, we began to talk and laugh. At one point, I drank cocoa from his thermos and laughed so hard that it shot out my nose and ran down my coat. I don't know when I fell asleep; I just remember the humming of the wheels rocking me to sleep.

It seemed like I had just shut my eyes when I woke to warm sunlight beaming through the windshield. Standing, I stretched and yawned and twisted my long hair up under my cap. Slinging my backpack over my shoulder I looked around for my jolly driver. The bus doors were open and I stepped into the cool morning air. He was gone. It was still cold outside. I crossed my arms and tried to shake off the chill. Slowly I made my way into the bus terminal. I was in Spokane. We must have driven all night. I sat down and looked through my last bit of change to call my sister to come pick me up. While I wandered around the terminal looking for a phone, I decided to go to the counter and ask about the bus driver. He had been so nice to me and I wanted to thank him.

"Hello," I said to the clerk.

"Yes, destination?" she asked.

"Oh," I stuttered. "I'm not going anywhere I just came in last night from Walla Walla."

The woman gave me a confused, hard stare.

"Anyway," I continued. "I was wondering if I could speak to the driver."

The woman rolled her eyes from me to her paperwork. Looking up she said, "No, no you couldn't have come in on that route, it must have been another bus. Let me see your ticket and I will see."

Puzzled, I began to search my backpack and I checked all my pockets. I couldn't find it.

"Shoot! I must have lost it," I said, shaking my head. "Really, that bus right over there." I pointed. Then I described the driver and our ride through the blizzard from Walla Walla.

The woman gave me a long hard look and said, "No you were not on that bus last night. You couldn't have been because the pass was closed. We didn't have any buses running that route last night." She stood and continued, "What are you up to anyway? Are you on drugs or something?" Confused, I started backing away from her. "Stay right there," she added. "I'm going to call someone."

I caught sight of the door, turned and ran. I ran and ran until I thought it was safe, stopping outside of a small convenience store. Sitting down on the slush-covered curb, I rested, with the bus ride running through my mind. I knew it was real. Otherwise, how did I get there? I could almost hear the driver's laugh as I looked down at the cocoa stain on my coat. I laughed and went to find a phone to call my sister.

She was happy and worried to hear from me, and said she would pick me up in a couple of hours.

As I waited I thought again about the jolly bus driver. Who was he really? I truly believe to this day that an angel drove that bus.

~Susan R. Boles

The Angel
in the Plaid Shirt

Angels and ministers of grace defend us.
~William Shakespeare

Was he an angel? More than twenty-five years later I remember him as plain as I remember what I had for breakfast this morning. Considering my poor memory these days, that's saying a lot.

My daughter was in school for the day. My husband Buck had just stormed out of the house after another disagreement, the nature of which I cannot recall. There were so many arguments those days. Much of our dissension revolved around his deteriorating health and trying to maintain our monument business while he continued to work full-time as a 911 dispatcher.

Two jobs were too physically demanding for him, and he wanted to quit working at the sheriff's office because the monument business was more lucrative. I protested because I felt the monument business, with all the lifting and hard manual labor, would soon be more than he could handle. Besides, if he weren't employed by the County Commission, he'd no longer have insurance. We needed the health insurance coverage desperately.

Buck had suffered a near heart attack; his cholesterol and triglyceride levels were astronomical, and he was diabetic. What I didn't know then was that in years to come he would need to have several amputations, would lose much of his eyesight, and go on dialysis.

On that warm spring day all those years ago, I cringed when the doorbell rang. We ran our monument business out of our house and I presumed this would be a customer. I brushed my hand across my cheek to wipe away a stray tear.

An older man, slightly bent and wearing a red plaid shirt and overalls, stood on the porch. I opened the door and invited him into the living room. I offered him a seat but he remained standing. He spoke in a calm deep voice that seemed to personify peace, but it was his eyes that totally mesmerized me. They were the bluest, deepest, calmest eyes I had ever seen. I could not look away.

He inquired about buying a monument and held up a brochure he had about our business. I offered to show him stones we had in the lot available for sale, but he declined. I am certain that throughout our conversation he noticed my red eyes and the sniffles I tried to hold back. Kindness and warmth radiated from this man and the comfort was almost more than I could bear at that dark moment in my life.

As he turned to go, his crystal eyes never left

my face. Before he closed the door behind him, he said, "It will all work out."

I cried more vigorously. Being in the presence of someone who made me feel consoled started my weeping once again. But this time it was different. The sobs were cleansing and renewing. I felt like all my worries had been washed away.

I never did tell my husband about my encounter with this man. Instead, I tried to remain quiet about what I thought he should do. A day or two later he said, "I've been thinking about what you said. I believe the best thing would be to sell the monument business and continue at the Sheriff's Office. That health insurance is more important than the extra money we would make with the tombstones."

A few months later, we sold the business. Through the years, Buck endured many hospital stays and spent the last years of his life in a nursing home. So, indeed, the insurance had been of utmost importance. Yet what I remember most from that time was the slightly stooped man dressed in farmer's attire who walked into my living room and led me beside the still waters.

An angel? He must have been. He soothed my troubled soul.

~Shirley Nordeck Short

Blue Bug Angel

In Heaven an angel is nobody in particular.
~George Bernard Shaw

I was the daughter that Aunt Bea never had. A childhood kidnapping and rape had left her barren. When my mother was diagnosed with cancer shortly after I was born, Aunt Bea cared for her. I was fourteen when Mama died. Various relatives invited me into their homes, but how could I leave Aunt Bea, who had cared for me since babyhood? Why would I want to live with people I barely knew? Aunt Bea needed me as much as I needed her.

When I grew up, I moved to Los Angeles. Aunt Bea remained in San Antonio running her own neighborhood grocery business. I worried nightly about my elderly aunt, on her own, on the wrong side of town, ringing up sales that barely supported her.

One night, later than I would have expected her to telephone, Aunt Bea called sounding breathless and anxious. I pictured my seventy-five-year-old aunt, 1,300 miles away, alone, vulnerable, pushing broken English to the limit when no one was around who understood her native Spanish.

Her voice trembled as she said, "Some boys came into the store. They stole sodas and beer from the cooler and ran out the door. I screamed at them to stop. I had to chase them."

"Where are you now?" I blurted out, near tears.

I pictured the meager cash register. I envisioned a cold hospital room—bandages!

"I'm in the living room. The police just left. The store's locked up."

"Are you hurt, Aunt Bea?"

"Just my knees," she replied with a moan. "My

legs gave out when I chased the boys. I fell to the ground and watched them disappear in the distance. I screamed at them and then looked up to the sky and prayed."

Thank God there had been no confrontation.

"Then I saw the girl," Aunt Bea said.

"There was a girl, too?" I gasped.

"She wasn't with the boys," Aunt Bea explained. "At first, I thought it was you. I didn't see her until I ran outside. Suddenly, she was lifting me up from the ground and asking me if I was all right."

Probably a customer, I thought. She must have seen the boys running from the store. That was bound to look suspicious.

"She never bought anything," Aunt Bea went on. "She just lifted me up, helped me inside and telephoned for help. When I finished talking to the police, she was gone."

It had probably been someone who hadn't wanted to get involved, I surmised. And she had probably thought that Aunt Bea was in no condition to conduct business after her ordeal. Of course, my aunt was always in condition to conduct business.

"What did she look like?" I asked, thinking I might remember her from the neighborhood.

"She was tall and slim," Aunt Bea began. "Her skin was very fair. She looked like an Americana. She had long light brown hair like yours. It fell straight across her back. I guess the little blue bug car that I saw parked alongside the store was hers. There was no one else around and no other cars stopped."

Thirteen hundred miles away in my California apartment, I sat in wonderment as I listened to Aunt Bea describe the girl who had helped her. I was tall and slim. I wore my golden brown hair long. Despite my Mexican roots, my skin was as fair as an Irish girl's. Anyone describing that girl might have described me. There was more.

When I had first moved to Los Angeles, I had fallen in love with the colorful profusion of Volkswagen Beetles. The little cars roamed the LA freeways like giant insects. Within a few months, I had traded in my cumbersome Pontiac for a cute sky blue bug. In San Antonio's hot, humid climate the radiator-free, air-cooled VW Beetles were as rare as snowstorms.

Thirteen hundred miles separated me from my beloved Aunt Bea. Yet someone who looked like me and who even drove the same kind of car as I did had appeared at my aunt's grocery store. This angel had helped Aunt Bea through the aftermath of a terrifying crime and ordeal. The angel had summoned help and then disappeared when the police arrived.

My beloved Aunt Bea passed away thirty years ago, but I still share this story with others. Inevitably, listeners smile and say, "That was an angel." I call it my Blue Bug Angel story.

~Susana Nevarez-Marquez

Ashley's Angel

Evening, morning and noon I will pray and
cry aloud and He shall hear my voice.
~Psalm 55:17

W hen my daughter turned nine-
teen, she announced to us she was
moving from our small mountain town in central California
to Pasadena. I wasn't crazy about my youngest
daughter moving to the big city, but I remembered
The Beach Boys song, "The Little Old Lady from
Pasadena." So if my daughter seemed determined
to relocate to southern California, that city seemed
like a safer choice than most.

After a couple of years of junior college, she

and her roommate, Laura, decided to transfer to the university. That meant moving away from the little old ladies in Pasadena. As starving college students they had to settle for a place that was less than advantageous—to say the least.

"We're not living in the ghetto. We're just living in the 'ghett,'" Ashley joked, trying to reassure us. She was right. It wasn't completely frightening, but there were just enough shady characters and siren sounds to keep a mother on her knees every night asking God to send angels to watch over the petite blonde beauty living in Los Angeles.

After parking her car one night, Ashley cautiously began walking to her door when she passed a group of guys who took notice of the fact she was alone. She and Laura had made a habit of calling each other as soon as they got out of the car and staying on the phone until they were safely inside, but tonight Laura wasn't home either. Pretending to be on the phone, Ashley heard footsteps following her. With her heart in her throat, she breathed a prayer for safety.

Within minutes, she heard a voice behind her. "Sweetie, you're being followed and I am just going to walk with you until you get to your door."

"Normally if some guy calls me 'sweetie,' he's the one I want to avoid," Ashley informed. "But the minute this man opened his mouth, I felt safe.

"He didn't actually walk with me," she informed me. "He stayed a few steps behind. I reached my apartment, put my key in the door, and turned to thank him, but he was gone. He hadn't had time to travel that far, but still he was nowhere in sight."

While Ashley didn't get to express her gratitude to her benefactor that night, I haven't stopped thanking God for answering this fretting mother's prayers.

~Linda Newton

Meet Our Contributors

Susan Boles lives with her husband of thirty-six years and their three spoiled dogs in Tyler, TX. Originally from the Pacific Northwest, she has enjoyed a lifetime of traveling and journaling all the stories of the treasures and lives she's met along the road -- true stories of life and love.

Pam Depoyan holds a B.A. degree in English from Loyola Marymount University, Los Angeles, CA. Working in corporate communications, she also writes freelance and has been published in Highlights for Children and Pray! She enjoys creating "word-photo stories" that inspire and encourage. Read more or e-mail her at www.wordglow.wordpress.com.

Tom Kaden is counselor at Someone To Tell It To — www.someonetotellitto.org. He is a graduate of Messiah College and Asbury Theological Seminary. Tom and his wife Sarah and their four children live in Carlisle, PA.

Mary Potter Kenyon has had over 300 articles and essays published in newspapers, magazines and anthologies, including four Chicken Soup for the Soul books. She conducts couponing and writing workshops for local colleges and writes a weekly column for Dubuque's Telegraph Herald. She blogs at marypotterkenyon.com. Learn more at marypotter-kenyon.writersresidence.com.

Lisa Leshaw has created a new "bucket list" that includes writing for a major magazine. Until then she is thrilled to spend her days on frog hunts with Mush and Gab and walks in the park with Stu (and eating tons of chocolate when no one is looking).

Michelle Close Mills' poetry and short stories have appeared in many poetry and short story anthologies including several in the Chicken Soup for the Soul series. Michelle resides in Central Florida with her husband, two kids, two meowing furbabies, and three chirping featherbabies. Learn more at www.authorsden.com/michelleclosemills.

Nell Musolf lives in Minnesota with her husband and two sons, and is always on the lookout for more angels in her life. E-mail Nell at nellmus@aol.com.

Susana Nevarez-Marquez is a lifelong observer of spiritual events. The sense of wonder that the Blue Bug incident provoked sparked an urge to write. Currently, she writes ethnic and romantic ction, all with a supernatural element inspired by true events. E-mail her at NevMarWrite@gmail.com.

Linda Newton is a counselor in California, and a

popular speaker at women's events. Visit her online at www.LindaNewtonSpeaks.com. She is author of 12 Ways to Turn Your Pain Into Praise, and Better Than Jewels.

Shirley Nordeck Short has been published in previous Chicken Soup for the Soul editions, Guideposts, Reader's Digest and local publications. She combines her two great loves by writing about the guinea pigs she rescues, and assures you if her guinea pigs could talk they'd have lots of angel stories to tell. E-mail her at shirleynshort@gmail.com.

Elisa Yager is a regular contributor to the Chicken Soup for the Soul series. When she's not writing, Elisa can be found doing something involving history, human resources, music or something in her church. Elisa would love to hear from you! E-mail her at author_ElisaYager@yahoo.com.

Meet Amy Newmark

Amy Newmark is the best-selling author, editor-in-chief, and publisher of the *Chicken Soup for the Soul* book series. Since 2008, she has published 140 new books, most of them national bestsellers in the U.S. and Canada, more than doubling the number of Chicken Soup for the Soul titles in print today. She is also the author of *Simply Happy*, a crash course in Chicken Soup for the Soul advice and wisdom that is filled with easy-to-implement, practical tips for having a better life.

Amy is credited with revitalizing the Chicken

Soup for the Soul brand, which has been a publishing industry phenomenon since the first book came out in 1993. By compiling inspirational and aspirational true stories curated from ordinary people who have had extraordinary experiences, Amy has kept the twenty-four-year-old Chicken Soup for the Soul brand fresh and relevant.

Amy graduated *magna cum laude* from Harvard University where she majored in Portuguese and minored in French. She then embarked on a three-decade career as a Wall Street analyst, a hedge fund manager, and a corporate executive in the technology field. She is a Chartered Financial Analyst.

Her return to literary pursuits was inevitable, as her honors thesis in college involved traveling throughout Brazil's impoverished northeast region, collecting stories from regular people. She is delighted to have come full circle in her writing career — from collecting stories "from the people" in Brazil as a twenty-year-old to, three decades later, collecting stories "from the people" for Chicken Soup for the Soul.

When Amy and her husband Bill, the CEO of Chicken Soup for the Soul, are not working, they are visiting their four grown children.

Follow Amy on Twitter @amynewmark. Listen to her free daily podcast, The Chicken Soup for the Soul Podcast, at www.chickensoup.podbean.com, or find it on iTunes, the Podcasts app on iPhone, or on your favorite podcast app on other devices.

Changing lives one story at a time®
www.chickensoup.com